Dedication

Photo by Margo Bors

Barbara M. Pitschel
1939-2010

Barbara Pitschel was Head Librarian of the Helen Crocker Russell Library of Horticulture. During her tenure, 1981-2010, the Library grew to become the most comprehensive horticultural library in northern California. She served on the Board of Directors and as President of the Council on Botanical and Horticultural Libraries and received its Charles Robert Long Award of Merit.

Barbara's involvement in the plant world went beyond her role as a librarian. She and her husband Roland were concerned and passionate about our native flora and were founding and lifetime members of the Yerba Buena Chapter of the California Native Plant Society. From creating programs to hosting board meetings to producing the chapter's newsletter, Barbara's care and commitment to excellence were evident. Barbara and Roland Pitschel were also leaders in the restoration work and planning that became the Bernal Hilltop Native Grassland Restoration Project, and were honored by the Trust for Public Land for their thirty years of volunteer park stewardship.

Barbara was passionate about botanical art, and the Library was the venue for rotating art exhibitions for the twenty-nine years she worked there. She purchased works of art from many of the shows. Her home was filled with a wonderful collection of botanical art, mostly works that featured the California native plants she loved so much.

More than anything, Barbara was a dedicated friend to many of us in the horticultural world and made every person feel special and appreciated. This art exhibition and catalog are dedicated to Barbara as a tribute to her and to honor her distinguished career.

Don Mahoney
Curator
San Francisco Botanical Garden Society

Made in the USA
Middletown, DE
19 June 2016

Treasures

from San Francisco Botanical Garden
at Strybing Arboretum

September 1 - December 30, 2011

Watercolor Paintings
by Mary L. Harden and her Master Artists

Juanita Alexander - Nancy J. Ballard - Roslyn Banish - Margaret Barr
Terese Bartholomew - Dianne Boate - Jo Boero - Linda Cavanaugh
Nancy Cohrs - Patricia Compton - Catherine Dellor - Yvonne Goldman
Michael Hanley - Mary Ann Ho - Jane Kraft - Lorry Luikart - Judy Mac
Martha McClaren - Peggy McIntyre - Dolores Morrison - Blue Murov
Rosemary O'Connell - Jill Petersen - Mary Plovanic - Stephanie Tarczy
Kate Townsend - Amber Turner - Katie Young

With Contributions
by San Francisco Botanical Garden Society

Don Mahoney - David Kruse-Pickler - Brandy Kuhl - Molley Lowry

Helen Crocker Russell Library of Horticulture
San Francisco Botanical Garden at Strybing Arboretum
Golden Gate Park
1199 Ninth Avenue
San Francisco, CA 94122

sfbg.org

First published 2011 by San Francisco Botanical Garden Society,
San Francisco, CA
on the occasion of the exhibition
Treasures from San Francisco Botanical Garden at Strybing Arboretum
Watercolor Paintings by Mary L. Harden and her Master Artists
Helen Crocker Russell Library of Horticulture
San Francisco Botanical Garden at Strybing Arboretum, Golden Gate Park
September 1- December 30, 2011

A catalog record for this book is available from the Library of Congress.

ISBN-13 978-0-615-57298-7
ISBN-10 0615572987

Printed by Craftsmen Printing, San Jose, CA.

Distributed by San Francisco Botanical Garden Society, San Francisco, CA.

Art direction by Mary L. Harden, MaryHardenDesigns.com
Front cover: *Banksia serrata* by Mary L. Harden
Back cover: *Treasures* Map © 2011 Mary L. Harden
Publication consultant and graphic design by Helene Sobol, HeleneSobol.com

Table of Contents

Introduction

More than two years ago, Mary Harden, with Barbara Pitschel's inspiration and encouragement, began to plan an exhibition for the Helen Crocker Russell Library of Horticulture. The exhibition would feature watercolor paintings of plants from San Francisco Botanical Garden. The artists, Mary's most accomplished students and Mary herself, would choose the plants they wished to paint after study and direct observation.

Barbara did not live to see the exhibition realized. *Treasures from San Francisco Botanical Garden at Strybing Arboretum,* the *Treasures* map, and this catalog are dedicated to her memory. They are a true labor of love – for the Botanical Garden, for Barbara, and for the wondrous beauty of plants as they exist in nature and in art.

Over the past months, Mary, her Master Artists and San Francisco Botanical Garden Society staff and volunteers have worked together to create the catalog and *Treasures* map to accompany and commemorate the exhibition. Mary also envisioned the catalog and map as documentation of the Botanical Garden's unique plant collections and as a special guide to walk the Garden paths. Mary's vision captured my imagination and took me directly to three senior staff members of the Botanical Garden Society – Don Mahoney, David Kruse-Pickler and Brandy Kuhl – who agreed to contribute to the project. Molley Lowry, our Art Exhibits Coordinator and longtime docent and volunteer, joined with them to develop most of the catalog's written content.

Treasures from San Francisco Botanical Garden, the exhibition, is presented for only four months. This catalog establishes a permanent record of Mary's educational and artistic contribution and the talent and generosity of her twenty-eight students. The catalog also provides botanical information about each of the plants they painted, as well as engaging Botanical Garden lore.

We sincerely believe and hope that all those who treasure San Francisco Botanical Garden and the world of plants will also treasure this catalog.

Sue Ann L. Schiff
Executive Director
San Francisco Botanical Garden Society

November 2011

The Exhibition

Treasures from San Francisco Botanical Garden follows two previous exhibitions that I have had the privilege of presenting for the Helen Crocker Russell Library of Horticulture: *Between Art and Science,* in 2006, and *Echoes of Darwin,* in 2009. In this 2011 exhibition I chose to focus on unusual, rare and extraordinary plants in the current collection. This exhibition blends two main aims of my Botanical Illustration Program: the depiction of a plant's beauty with taxonomical accuracy and the use of advanced watercolor techniques to create strong three-dimensionality.

The exhibition showcases the talents of artists who have studied with me and have become Master Artists in my program, progressing through several years of structured curriculum that includes precise rendering from life in graphite and colored pencil, in pen and ink, with quills, in gouache, and, in the most personal and immediate of media, translucent watercolor. Carefully designed layouts invite viewers to imagine the whole of a plant's structure while simultaneously examining the tiniest detail in sharp focus. The blending of these botanical art techniques with personal verve – that powerful force that lifts a two-dimensional object off the page and into our imagination – can be seen and felt throughout the thirty-piece exhibition.

Stylistic differences among the artists are united by our unique naturalist's watercolor palette, which, interestingly, contains no green pigments. The hundreds of greens in these artworks were created by spontaneously floating yellow, blue and red paint onto wet paper. Using this same technique and palette, I designed a special map for a walking tour to accompany the exhibition. Visitors can identify a favorite plant in the exhibition and locate it within the Botanical Garden. The map of the grounds, in a myriad of transparent greens, uses thumbnail versions of the paintings to show where the plants can be found, their places marked by numbered orange signs.

The work in this exhibition heralds an approach to botanical art that is not often seen: one that exalts plant matter as it exists within an ecosystem, with all of its holes, rips, insect bites, dried leaves, withered blossoms, and empty seed pods. Including these vivid examples of botanical characteristics within a fully realized narrative of a plant's life-cycle gives the viewer a realistic picture of the diversity of plants, and a more compelling and memorable visual image. Within this framework, each artist's rendering presents a wondrously personal view of a treasured plant in this year, in these seasons, and in the remarkable San Francisco Botanical Garden.

Mary L. Harden
Curator, *Treasures from San Francisco Botanical Garden at Strybing Arboretum*
Director, Mary L. Harden Botanical Illustration Program

The Garden

San Francisco Botanical Garden at Strybing Arboretum is located on fifty-five acres in Golden Gate Park. More than eight thousand different kinds of plants from around the world are displayed, organized primarily according to geographic areas with emphasis on the five mediterranean climate zones of the world – Coastal California, Central Chile, Southwest Australia, the Cape Province of South Africa and the Mediterranean basin.

When William Hammond Hall made the original plan for Golden Gate Park in 1872, he envisioned an arboretum and botanical garden for San Francisco. By 1890, Park Superintendent John McLaren had identified the location for the arboretum, and by the mid-1890s, had begun planting conifers on the proposed site. The arboretum became a reality when Helene Strybing left a bequest to the City and County of San Francisco, providing that an arboretum and botanical garden be established. Work began in 1937 from a plan formulated by McLaren and Eric Walther, the newly appointed director of the arboretum. San Francisco Botanical Garden officially opened as Strybing Arboretum in 1940. Over the years, many others have added to Helene Strybing's generous founding gift to create a botanical garden of great beauty and importance.

The Bay Area's mild temperatures, wet winters and dry summers, coupled with frequent summer coastal fog, provide a range of climatic conditions that exist in few other botanical gardens in the world. With its unique microclimate, the Botanical Garden is able to recreate conditions of the cloud forests of Central and South America and Southeast Asia. Rare high elevation palms as well as plants from New Zealand and temperate Asia also thrive here. Largely due to these natural advantages, the Botanical Garden is known for its unique, diverse and significant botanical collections. The extensive *Magnolia* collection, attracting visitors with its dazzling display of winter flowers, is recognized as the world's fourth most important collection of *Magnolia* for conservation purposes – and the most important outside China, where a majority of *Magnolia* species are found.

San Francisco Botanical Garden's twenty-six gardens include, among others, the Redwood Grove, Succulent Garden, Ancient Plant Garden, Garden of Fragrance, Moon Viewing Garden, John Muir Nature Trail, Zellerbach Garden, Camellia Garden, Rhododendron Garden and Children's Garden.

The Botanical Garden Society

In 1954, the friends and associates of Arboretum director Eric Walther helped to establish the Strybing Arboretum Society to support the continued development of the Botanical Garden and to provide educational programs. In 2004, Strybing Arboretum changed its name to San Francisco Botanical Garden at Strybing Arboretum, and the Arboretum Society followed suit, becoming San Francisco Botanical Garden Society at Strybing Arboretum.

The mission of the Botanical Garden Society is to build communities of support for the Garden and cultivate the bond between people and plants. The Botanical Garden Society works in partnership with the San Francisco Recreation and Park Department to welcome annually more than 200,000 visitors from San Francisco, the Bay Area and all over the world.

With the help of its members, donors and more than five hundred volunteers who contribute their time and energy to virtually every facet of the Garden, the Botanical Garden Society funds Garden improvements, provides curatorial and plant collections management services, and propagates plants for the Garden and for sale to the public. It also operates the Helen Crocker Russell Library of Horticulture, provides docent training and daily guided walks, serves ten thousand children a year through its youth education program, sponsors other educational and community programming, and manages the Garden Bookstore.

The Library

Helen Crocker Russell Library of Horticulture

The Helen Crocker Russell Library of Horticulture is northern California's most comprehensive horticultural library and serves as one of the major horticultural-botanical libraries in the western United States, attracting over 20,000 visitors per year. The Library is funded and operated by San Francisco Botanical Garden Society, with the support of private donors and foundations. Located inside the Main Gate of the Botanical Garden, the Library was presented by the Botanical Garden Society (formerly Strybing Arboretum Society) to the City and County of San Francisco for public use and inspiration at a dedication ceremony in April 1972.

The Library's holdings include over 27,000 volumes, including a rare book collection housed in a temperature and humidity controlled room, 350 plant and garden periodicals, current and retrospective nursery and seed catalogs, a pamphlet file, historical slides and a small collection of garden videos. Other features include a 1,600-volume children's botanical library, children's story time programs and botanical art exhibitions. The Library's collections cover all aspects of horticulture, including gardening, garden design, botanical art, ethnobotany and pest management, with an emphasis on plants grown in mediterranean and other mild temperate climates. Library staff is assisted by a knowledgeable group of over thirty volunteers.

Early in its history the Library began to exhibit artwork related to botany, horticulture and the natural world. The art exhibitions have become a regular part of the Library's programming, with rotating shows on display throughout the year. Recognized for promoting interest in botanical art, the Library has served as the venue for presenting well-known artists as well as encouraging the work of talented beginners. Exhibitions have included a variety of artistic mediums such as watercolor paintings, hand-colored etchings, photography, pen and ink drawings, and collections of antique botanical illustration.

Brandy Kuhl
Head Librarian
Helen Crocker Russell Library of Horticulture
San Francisco Botanical Garden Society

The Plants

Numbers correspond to plant locations shown on map.

 1. *Cupressus macrocarpa* – Monterey cypress
 2. *Himalayacalamus hookerianus* – Blue bamboo
 3. *Magnolia stellata* 'Waterlily' – Star magnolia
 4. *Magnolia stellata* 'Rosea' – Star magnolia
 5. *Camellia x williamsii* 'George Blandford' – Camellia
 6. *Chamaecyparis funebris* – False cypress
 7. *Bocconia arborea* – Plume poppy
 8. *Magnolia doltsopa* – Chinese magnolia, sweet michelia
 9. *Ginkgo biloba* – Maidenhair tree
10. *Phyllostachys nigra* 'Bory' – Snakeskin bamboo
11. *Magnolia dealbata* – Cloud forest magnolia
12. *Ardisia venosa* – Coralberry
13. *Chiranthodendron pentadactylon* – Mexican hand tree
14. *Metasequoia glyptostroboides* – Dawn redwood
15. *Garrya elliptica* – Coast silk tassel
16. *Fremontodendron* 'California Glory'– Flannel bush
17. *Colletia paradoxa* – Anchor plant
18. *Lapageria rosea* – Chilean bellflower
19. *Brugmansia sanguinea* – Red angel's trumpet
20. *Syzygium smithii* – Lilly pilly tree
21. *Banksia serrata* – Old man banksia
22. *Camellia reticulata* 'Notre Dame' – Camellia
23. *Protea* 'Pink Ice' – Protea
24. *Leucadendron argenteum* – Silver tree
25. *Leptospermum scoparium* cv. – New Zealand tea tree
26. *Metrosideros excelsa* – New Zealand Christmas tree
27. *Araucaria araucana* – Monkey puzzle tree
28. *Gunnera tinctoria* – Chilean rhubarb
29. *Magnolia grandiflora* – Southern magnolia
30. *Rhododendron* 'John McLaren' – Rhododendron

Treasures

from
San Francisco
Botanical Garden
at Strybing Arboretum

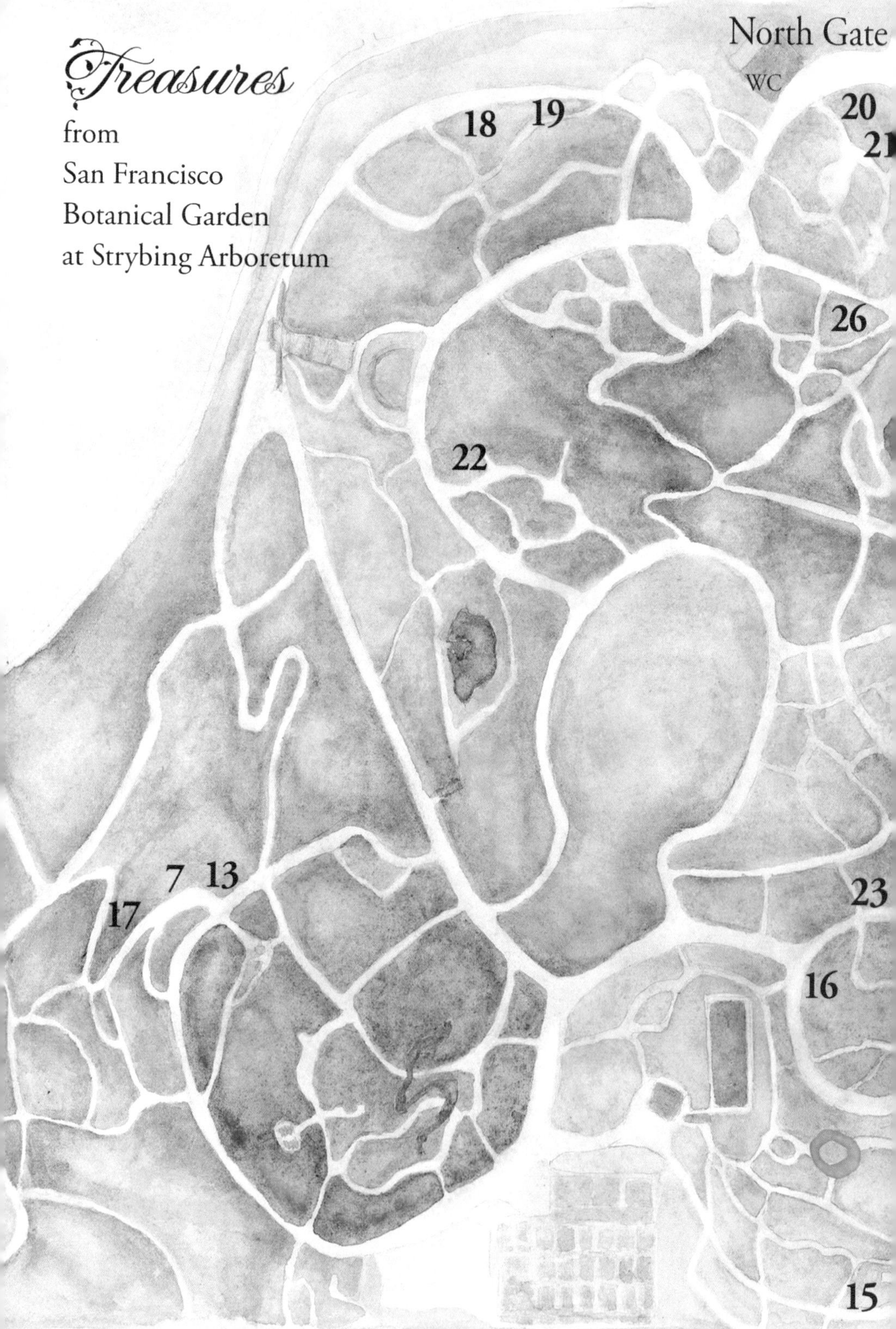

North Gate

WC

18   19

20

21

26

22

7   13

17

23

16

15

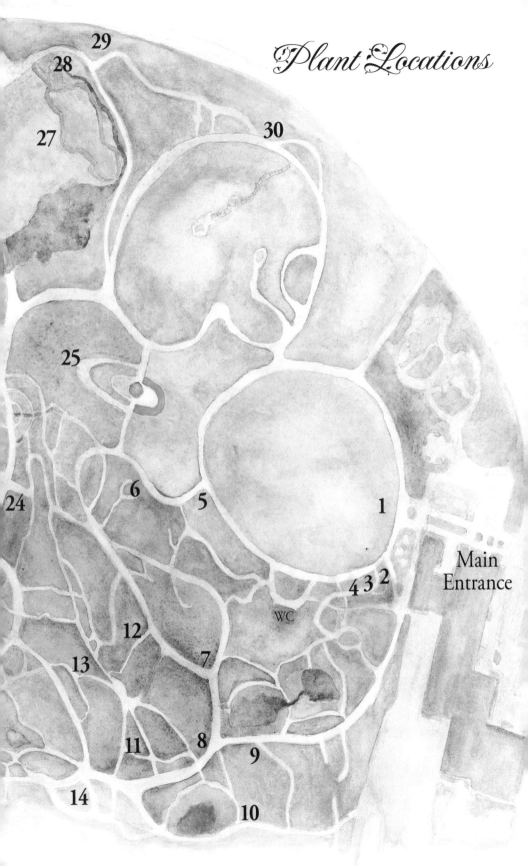

Plant Locations

Main
Entrance

1. Cupressus macrocarpa

Monterey cypress
Native to California

The Monterey cypress standing tall in the Great Meadow welcomes everyone to the Botanical Garden with its raised branches and its majesty. This tree is drawn by each of Mary's students during our very first class to push us past our fears. In sun or fog the tree shows its history shaped by the passage of time and the winds of the Pacific Ocean.

Martha McClaren *Artist*

The Monterey cypress is one of the three major canopy trees in Golden Gate Park. This species, along with the Monterey pine and the blue gum eucalyptus, were among the first trees planted when the Park was being established in the 1870s. The cypress is the most prevalent of these and the most variable in appearance. Many mature trees line the entrances and avenues in Golden Gate Park. Often seen from afar as silhouettes, their dark foliage creates a dramatic contrast to the blue or grey sky. Closer to Ocean Beach, they take on a severe windswept character that is quite picturesque, as seen along much of the central and northern California coastline.

One of the most majestic and regal specimens of *Cupressus macrocarpa* can be found just inside the Main Gate of the Botanical Garden in the Great Meadow. This is considered the Garden's flagship tree, serving as a constant reminder that our history is firmly rooted as an arboretum. When planted in watered lawns, Monterey cypresses grow very fast and reach sizes not seen in their natural habitat. Our mature trees are all well over one hundred years old. Many of these mature Monterey cypresses, in the Botanical Garden and throughout Golden Gate Park, are nearing the end of their lifespan. In recent years, a few have been toppled and lost in nearly every major winter storm. Sadly, due to storms, our flagship tree has lost several lower limbs.

Cupressus macrocarpa has been extensively planted and naturalized throughout the world as a timber tree. Along with the Monterey pine *(Pinus radiata)*, the trees are grown in large plantations in South America and Africa. Naturally occurring populations have always been rare. Only two groves of *C. macrocarpa* now exist in Monterey County.

2. Himalayacalamus hookerianus

Blue bamboo
Native to the Himalayas

For me, the enduring importance of art is to delight and surprise, and to enlarge my world. Art allows me to see and think in new ways, to make a dying leaf a universe, and a root a star. When I was first introduced to blue bamboo in the Botanical Garden, I realized that I had walked past it many times without really seeing it. The striking, dusty blue color dazzled me. As I spent more time with the plant, I began to appreciate the array of colors and designs within a single clump. This world of surprising color and design is what I sought to capture in my painting, and to offer to viewers.

Kate Townsend *Artist*

Blue bamboo is named for a thick blue wax that looks like powder, appearing on new shoots in the spring. The wax turns mostly yellow-green after the first year, but retains a slightly bluish hue at the base of each culm (stem). This beautiful bamboo can be found in the Temperate Asia collection. As its botanical name implies, it is native to the Himalayas, from India to Bhutan.

Although some bamboos grow as tall as trees, they are all in the grass family (Poaceae). Bamboo is also one of the fastest growing plants; some species are known to grow as much as thirty-nine inches in twenty-four hours. While bamboos are found around the world, they are most commonly associated with Asia, where they are used for everything from building construction to cooking.

Himalayacalamus hookerianus is relatively new to horticulture in the United States. The few that were being grown before 1990 flowered in the early 1990's and then produced seed. Many bamboo species exhibit mass flowering, with all plants in a population flowering simultaneously. This first generation of blue bamboo plants can grow as tall as twenty feet with culms measuring an inch across. Many of the second generation seedlings appear to be smaller growing plants. Consequently, there are selections of mini-forms now on the market. Several of these mini-forms are planted in the Botanical Garden, but given limited experience with their growing patterns, their eventual size is uncertain. A clumping bamboo whose new shoots appear near the base of the plant, this relatively hardy species is destined to be popular for its manageable growth and exquisite coloration.

3. *Magnolia stellata* 'Waterlily'

Star magnolia
Species native to Japan

The branches of Magnolia stellata 'Waterlily' are bare and linear in winter. I started my painting in January with a cutting that was dry, intricate and calligraphic. Later, I painted a second section, with the woody parts plumper and colorful buds emerging. Finally, a star-like flower opened and small bits of green showed here and there. I visited this plant every week for three months, observing its slowly changing growth pattern and enjoying the experience of discovery.

Mary Plovanic *Artist*

Star magnolias are popular small trees for residential gardens. There are many cultivars. *Magnolia stellata* 'Waterlily' is well known, fragrant, and valued for its showy tepals (petals and sepals) – more than twice the number of many other star magnolias. Our specimen in the Temperate Asia collection, near the sidewalk bordering the Great Meadow, is quite mature and large for this cultivar. The pink buds open to white flowers on bare branches each winter in a very layered and lacey display.

The Botanical Garden is home to an important collection of magnolias. The earliest plantings date from the 1930's and include the first *Magnolia campbellii* to bloom in the United States. *Magnolia campbellii* is considered to be one of the most beautiful of the Asian magnolias. It has large ten-inch pink flowers that bloom on bare branches covering the trees for almost a month. With a dozen or more mature trees in the Botanical Garden, they can be seen when they are flowering from almost any vantage point. Many species of *Magnolia* have been added over the years so that San Francisco Botanical Garden is now recognized internationally for its conservation of *Magnolia* species.

4. *Magnolia stellata* 'Rosea'

Star magnolia

Species native to Japan

Magnolia stellata 'Rosea' captured my attention in springtime. I was drawn to its plethora of pale blossoms – with petals dancing and drooping in all directions – against a bold, branching structure. I wanted to capture the lightness and energy of this particular magnolia.

Roslyn Banish *Artist*

Magnolia stellata, also known as the star magnolia, is a slow growing shrub or small tree. The species is listed as endangered in its native habitat of moist open forests in Japan. It is deciduous, with flowers appearing on leafless branches in late winter or early spring. If the weather is warm enough, the specimens in the Botanical Garden have been known to have a few flowers open on New Year's Day. The species is named star magnolia for the ten to thirty narrow, white strap-shaped tepals (petals and sepals) that radiate out like a star. Star magnolia flowers have the largest number of tepals of all the magnolias. The flowers have a sweet fragrance and develop unusual seed pods. A mature, established tree can be covered with thousands of flowers, really lighting up a woodland garden, especially when combined with colorful spring bulbs.

The Botanical Garden is fortunate to have three mature specimens (two cultivars and one species), each approaching fifty years old and twenty feet tall, which is considered large for *M. stellata*. The cultivars 'Rosea' (illustrated here) and 'Waterlily' (previous illustration) are located past the Library in the Temperate Asia collection. The *M. stellata* species is located just west of the Garden's Nursery and should not be missed.

5. *Camellia* x *williamsii* 'George Blandford'

Camellia

Garden origin: Caerhays Castle, Cornwall, England

*I painted this camellia because the delicate pink flower reveals grace, innocence,
beauty, femininity and strength – all elements that I admire in women.*

Katie Young *Artist*

San Francisco Botanical Garden began developing a major collection of
camellias early in its history. Since 1978, the Garden's collection has almost
tripled, growing from 124 to 346 different camellias, including 45 species.
Among these specimens is a group called the *Camellia* x *williamsii* hybrids,
which were developed by J. C. Williams and Mary Christian at Caerhays
Castle in Cornwall, England in the 1930's. The cultivar illustrated here,
'George Blandford', was named after one of the head gardeners. These hybrids
between *C. japonica* and *C. saluenensis* were considered a breakthrough in
camellia breeding as they had the cold hardiness of *C. japonica* and flowered
at a young age like *C. saluenensis*. They are also known for producing flowers
in abundance and for shedding them once they are spent, a highly desired
quality that keeps the plants fresh-looking and clean. There is no need for a
gardener to deadhead or remove the spent flowers. As the plants mature and
reach heights up to eight feet, their branches become pendulous, creating a
lovely downward cascade of flowers.

The cultivar 'George Blandford' was introduced in 1962 and won a Royal
Horticultural Society Award of Garden Merit in 2002. The semi-double
flowers are a rich pink with darker tones and appear in abundance for many
weeks in early to mid-spring. The Botanical Garden's only specimen was
planted in 1967. It is growing with many other camellias and magnolias just
off the southeast side of the Great Meadow.

6. Chamaecyparis funebris

False cypress

Native to China

I was captivated by the somber, stooped form of Chamaecyparis funebris. *Could its soulful demeanor be the result of its burdensome common names – false cypress, Chinese weeping cypress and mourning cypress – or is it a much deeper and wiser calling? This plant is definitely worthy of further investigation.*

Jo Boero *Artist*

Chamaecyparis funebris is a graceful conifer often described as mysterious or sorrowful, giving rise to the Latin name funebris, meaning funeral. One of its common names is the mourning cypress. The branches are pendulous for ten feet or more, which gives a weeping appearance to the tree. It has a wide distribution in China where it has been planted near temples, monasteries and tombs for thousands of years. This species of *Chamaecyparis* is one of the hardiest, often found covered by snow. It will grow in almost any soil but is probably best suited for parks or large estates because it grows too large for small gardens. There are a few specimens in the Botanical Garden, all planted in 1986; the tallest is now about thirty feet high.

The false cypress, Chinese weeping cypress, or funeral cypress has had many common and scientific names over the years. Botanists from China have placed it in the genus *Cupressus* while other botanists continue to keep it in the genus *Chamaecyparis.* Taxonomic revisions of plant lineages are ongoing and we can expect to see changes to many plant names in the future as molecular studies reveal more information about relationships among plants.

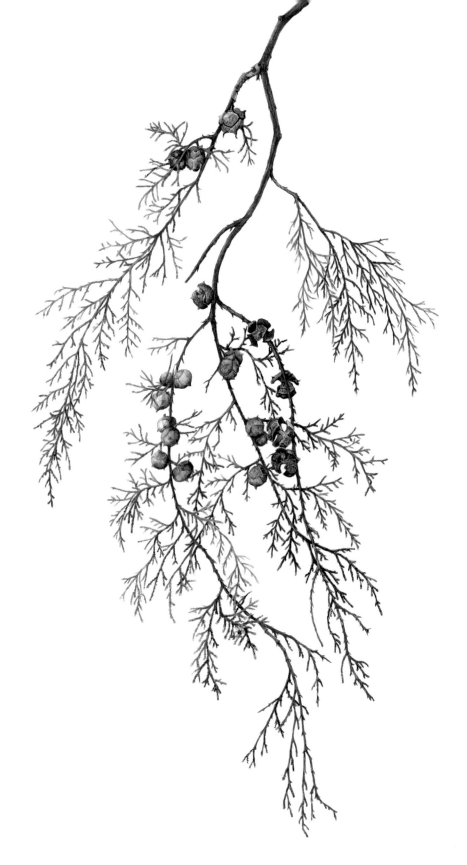

7. Bocconia arborea

Plume poppy
Native to Mexico and Central America

*As I wandered the Botanical Garden in search of a special specimen to paint,
I became aware of the loveliness of the* Bocconia arborea. *Looking closely,
I saw the intricate beauty of all of the elements of its life cycle in sharp focus.
I return again and again to this marvelous and complex plant, which I had
previously passed on the path without noticing.*

Stephanie Tarczy *Artist*

Looking at this shrub or small tree, one might never guess that it is in the
poppy family. Called plume poppy, the individual flowers do not look like
typical poppies, but are tiny and greenish-white, lack petals, and appear
in large hanging racemes that are up to ten inches long. The deeply lobed
leaves are about ten inches long, with a grey-green upper surface and silvery
underside. The fruit ripens to reveal small egg-shaped black and red seeds
hanging in large clusters, or "plumes," that last several months.

Bocconia arborea is native to the cloud forests of southern Mexico extending
into Central America. Cloud forests are high elevation montane habitats
rich with vegetation and species diversity. Their cool temperatures and almost
constant cloud cover are similar to the San Francisco climate, particularly
in Golden Gate Park. San Francisco Botanical Garden is one of the only
botanical gardens that can grow this *Bocconia* successfully outdoors outside
its native habitat. *Bocconia arborea* is very rare in cultivation.

The Garden's oldest plume poppy, growing on the edge of the Succulent
Garden, is a twenty-foot-tall tree with multiple trunks, some measuring
twelve inches in diameter. Planted more than fifty years ago, this particular
plant has survived many cold winters even though the species is described
as being frost sensitive. It is known to have survived a very cold week in
1989, when temperatures were below freezing for five days. Many younger
specimens can be found growing with other companion plant species in the
Mesoamerican Cloud Forest.

8. *Magnolia doltsopa*

Chinese magnolia, sweet michelia

Native to the eastern Himalayas

This huge and gorgeous old tree produces masses of lively downward-growing blossoms in brilliant white. White presents a dilemma to a watercolorist because despite the absence of apparent color, the full color spectrum must be revealed in very pale, transparent washes.

Jane Kraft *Artist*

Magnolia doltsopa is undoubtedly one of the most beautiful trees in the Botanical Garden. The sweet fragrance from the multitude of flowers that cover each tree fills the air in late winter through spring. The flowers are abundant and visually stunning from a distance; up close, the individual large white flowers are elegant. In winter, the flower buds appear furry, with perfect warm coats to protect them from cold temperatures and also from chewing insects. This "fur" actually consists of bronze hairs covering the stipules that enclose each bud. The flower consists of white tepals, a term used when both petals and sepals are undifferentiated. The twelve to sixteen tepals radiate from a yellow center of spirally-arranged, relatively primitive reproductive parts. Plants in the magnolia family are believed to be some of the earliest flowering plants.

Native to subtropical Asia, *M. doltsopa* is relatively hardy and can be found planted up and down the West Coast, easily surviving temperatures in the low teens. In Yunnan Province of China, they can be as tall as ninety feet. At San Francisco Botanical Garden, they have reached a height of about fifty feet in the sixty years since they were planted. These are some of the larger specimens in cultivation in California. The species is quite variable and smaller forms make perfect street trees. There are many such street trees in neighborhoods adjacent to Golden Gate Park. Only fifteen feet tall after forty years, they are prolific bloomers.

The Botanical Garden has five mature specimens located in the Mesoamerican Cloud Forest, Southeast Asian Cloud Forest and the Moon Viewing Garden. Their blooming periods vary. While most are evergreen, one tree in the Mesoamerican Cloud Forest, adjacent to the Great Meadow, is deciduous during cold winters.

9. Ginkgo biloba

Maidenhair tree
Native to China

Many years ago I was given a silver leaf pin with delicately etched veins radiating from the stem to the outer edge like a fan. I prized it but never considered the source for the design. Much later, walking under a canopy of street trees, I looked up to see a golden multitude of my silver pins dancing in the breeze. I have wanted to paint those leaves ever since.

Juanita Alexander *Artist*

Ginkgo biloba, with its distinctive fan-shaped leaves, is perhaps one of the world's most recognized and revered trees. Botanists are not entirely sure where it originated. The fossil record indicates that the ginkgo was once widespread, but now is native only to China and even in China, known only in cultivation. *Ginkgo biloba* is a modern representative of an ancient lineage that predates flowering plants. Cultivated in China for several thousand years, the oldest, most majestic trees are often associated with shrines and temples. Some trees are more than one hundred sixty feet tall, and are estimated to be more than two thousand years old.

Today, ginkgos are often planted as street trees because they tolerate pollution, are hardy and have beautiful yellow fall color. Trees are either male or female. Male trees are usually planted as ornamentals since the female seed cones have an unpleasant smell. Female trees are, however, sometimes planted for their edible large seeds found within a fleshy coating. Extracts of the leaves are purported to enhance memory and have other health benefits. The plants are very resilient. In Japan, six trees within a mile of the Hiroshima nuclear blast were among the few living things to survive. The denuded trees eventually resprouted and are still alive today.

There are numerous specimens in the Ancient Plant Garden and one particularly beautiful tree in the Temperate Asia collection across from Anelli Pond. This tree, planted in 1973, arches over a dark-foliaged conifer; in autumn, the yellow leaves fall onto the almost black foliage, creating a striking image that lasts for several weeks.

10. *Phyllostachys nigra* 'Bory'

Snakeskin bamboo
Species native to China

Walking through the bamboo grove is a lovely experience. The path is narrow and cool. Many varieties are named, each is unique, and the nearness of the bamboo creates a dense, green forest of slender canes. The snakeskin bamboo is very tall, and it evokes a feeling of amazing strength in the thick column-like stems that climb to a canopy of feathery leaves. The origin of its common name is revealed in the reptilian blotches of dark green to purple-black that spread over patches of umber and rust. Bamboo has been a favorite of mine for many years and was a complete joy to paint.

Rosemary O'Connell *Artist*

The timber bamboos of China and Japan have been an important part of human history for millennia. The black bamboos, forms of *Phyllostachys nigra,* have been used extensively for furniture, musical instruments and building structures. The new shoots are edible.

In the cultivar 'Bory', the new shoots emerge green and then, instead of turning black as in other black bamboos, the stalks become spotted and streaked with dramatic dark brown patches. This unusual coloring is reflected in the common name, snakeskin bamboo. Growing to fifty feet tall in the wild, the 'Bory' is a running bamboo, its new shoots emerging up to ten feet or more from the parent plant. This requires careful management in any garden. Most home gardeners choose to plant bamboos that are categorized as clumping, since they are less invasive, their shoots growing in close proximity to the parent.

At the Botanical Garden, there is a grove of *P. nigra* 'Bory' that is twenty feet wide and fifty feet long, growing with many other bamboos, which together create a small bamboo forest. A quiet walking path around the Bamboo Pond provides a wonderful opportunity to experience what it might be like to be immersed in a bamboo forest. For both children and adults, it is a magical experience to stroll through this grove.

11. Magnolia dealbata

Cloud forest magnolia
Native to Mexico

Walking on a grey, wet fall day in the Botanical Garden, I rounded the corner to the Mesoamerican Cloud Forest, and there at my feet were several giant, magnificent leaves of the Magnolia dealbata *dressed in their autumnal colors and waiting to be painted. Later that spring, the seed-head appeared. What a gift.*

Amber Turner *Artist*

Magnolias have a worldwide distribution occurring in widely separated geographic areas, referred to by botanists as disjunct populations. They are native to Asia (mostly China), Central and South America, Mexico, the Caribbean and the southeastern United States. The few species in southern Mexico are cloud forest trees, including *Magnolia dealbata.* Closely related to *Magnolia macrophylla,* the big leaf magnolia of the southeastern United States, *M. dealbata* has even bigger leaves – twelve inches long and eight inches wide, perhaps the largest in the genus. The leaves have very persistent veins and become skeletonized after sitting on the forest floor for a few months. The leaf skeletons, or "ghost leaves" as they are sometimes called, are fascinating and can be considered natural works of art.

Listed as endangered in the wild due to habitat destruction, populations of *Magnolia dealbata* are limited to southern Mexico. There are three trees in the Mesoamerican Cloud Forest, two of which produce a few flowers each year. The flowers are large, as much as twelve inches in diameter, but last for just one day. These two trees, planted in 1986, are still quite young; the tallest is about thirty feet. Nearly unknown in cultivation, this is one of the rarest magnolias in the Botanical Garden's collection. To aid in its conservation, efforts are underway to propagate this species for more plantings in the Garden and other botanical gardens.

Internationally recognized for its emphasis on *Magnolia* conservation, the Botanical Garden currently has fifty-one species and thirty-five cultivars of *Magnolia.*

12. Ardisia venosa

Coralberry
Native to Mexico and Guatemala

I always stress that artists must fall in love with the plants they select in order to paint with passion. Hidden deep within the Mesoamerican Cloud Forest, I discovered the coralberry, and was struck by an eye-catching, huge, glowing mass of pink, red, coral, green, purple and black berries, firmly yet delicately held by an intricate structure of curving stems. Just imagine the great mass of pink flowers that must have preceded these extraordinary berries.

Mary L. Harden *Artist*

In the fall, a highlight of the Mesoamerican Cloud Forest is the strikingly beautiful *Ardisia venosa*. This twenty-year-old plant is about fifteen feet tall and fifteen feet wide, and blooms profusely for several months in the fall and winter. The floral display is followed by a profusion of dark red to purple-black fruits hanging like clusters of grapes. The individual flowers are pendulous, one-half inch long, and bell-shaped with petals that are bright ruby-rose with white reflexed tips and edges. Practically unknown in cultivation, this plant is positioned to become one of the best horticultural introductions for mild climates in recent years.

Native to the mountains of southern Mexico and Guatemala, this large shade-tolerant shrub would probably suffer in a hard frost, although its cold tolerance has not yet been fully tested. If the flowers appear to look like small hanging primroses, it is not too surprising. Recent molecular studies indicate that *Ardisia* and other plants in the Myrsinaceae family are now all placed in Primulaceae, the primrose family.

The Botanical Garden has two coralberry plants in the Mesoamerican Cloud Forest. The seeds for these plants were collected in Chiapas, Mexico by Dr. Dennis Breedlove, former Curator of Botany at the California Academy of Sciences. Many of the Mesoamerican Cloud Forest plants came from Dr. Breedlove's collecting trips to Chiapas in the 1970's and 1980's. Botanical Garden Society Curator Don Mahoney and Plant Collections Registrar Mona Bourell joined Dr. Breedlove on expeditions to Chiapas.

13. Chiranthodendron pentadactylon

Mexican hand tree
Native to Mexico and Guatemala

When I took my first pen and ink class from Mary L. Harden, I was given a dried Chiranthodendron pentadactylon *flower to draw. I was fascinated by the complex details, especially the five-fingered stamen. I drew the flower from several angles; each time I discovered a different view. The Mexican hand tree became my favorite subject as I progressed from pencil drawings to pen and ink to watercolor paintings. I followed the plant as it changed through the seasons and found the different stages of the developing fruits equally intriguing. When I was asked to create a painting for the exhibit, there was no question which plant I would pick.*

Mary Ann Ho *Artist*

Chiranthodendron pentadactylon, known variously as Mexican hand tree, monkey hand tree, and devil's hand tree, is called árbol de la manita (little hand tree) in southern Mexico. Quite impressive in its native habitat, mature specimens can be over one hundred feet tall. In cultivation, trees have reached a height of about sixty feet. This fast growing tree is not common in cultivation. Coastal California is the only known area where it is grown outside its native habitat.

As suggested by its many common names, *C. pentadactylon* has extraordinary flowers. With two-inch-long red stamens protruding from a large maroon cup-shaped structure comprised of sepals, they resemble five crimson fingers on a maroon hand. The yellow pollen appears to glow in contrast to the red flower. The flower, held upright on the branch, is full of sweet nectar and collects rainwater, making it attractive to visiting birds. The large, drooping, maple-like leaves have fuzzy brown wool-like trichomes (hairs) on the underside. The flowers are followed by five-inch long ridged fruits, also covered with small brown trichomes, which split into five lobes when dry. These capsules are spectacularly strange looking and nearly as intriguing as the Mexican hand tree's unique flower.

The Garden's oldest plant is located in the Succulent Garden. It produces no fruits, while newer plantings in the Mesoamerican Cloud Forest and one large tree bordering the South Terrace of the County Fair Building are very productive, yielding many large fruits and viable seed. Recently placed in the hibiscus family (Malvaceae), *C. pentadactylon* is closely related to the yellow-flowered flannel bush, *Fremontodendron,* which is native to California. A newly created hybrid named x *Chiranthofremontia lenzii* has yellow flowers with a reduced form of the "hand," and can be found growing in the Entry Garden near the Main Gate.

14. *Metasequoia glyptostroboides*

Dawn redwood
Native to central China

Metasequoia glyptostroboides is the botanical name I was most proud to learn in a plant identification class. It flows off the tongue. The tree itself has a beautiful, graceful appearance. I love that it is a particular rarity: a deciduous conifer. I worried that I would not be able to create an interesting painting of a green branch until I found this gorgeous specimen with catkins loaded with tiny new cones. Worries vanished.

Catherine Dellor *Artist*

Dawn redwoods are impressive trees with large fluted trunks that resemble the bald cypress, another deciduous member of the redwood family. Like the bald cypress, the dawn redwood grows best in moist habitats. The soft delicate foliage turns gold to russet in fall. When new growth appears in spring, it is tinged with pink. This fast growing tree can reach over one hundred fifty feet tall.

In the mid-1940's, *Metasequoia glyptostroboides* was discovered by Chinese botanists in a remote part of China and recognized as a living fossil previously thought to be extinct for twenty million years. Scientists in China consulted Ralph W. Chaney, a paleobotanist at the University of California, Berkeley, about their discovery, and sent specimens and eventually seeds to the Arnold Arboretum at Harvard. In 1948, Chaney and Milton Silverman, the science editor for the *San Francisco Chronicle,* became the first westerners to make the difficult journey to see the trees, returning with additional seeds and a few seedlings. The discovery of what was thought to be an extinct tree made headlines around the world. Recognizing that the average reader would struggle with the botanical name, Silverman and his editorial department named it the "Dawn Redwood." Grown from those first seeds and cuttings, the dawn redwood has become a common sight in botanical gardens and universities around the world.

The earliest plantings in the Botanical Garden are from 1950, from seeds distributed by the Arnold Arboretum, and are among the oldest in the United States. They can be found in the Temperate Asia collection, Ancient Plant Garden and the Redwood Grove. The most impressive stand is just southeast of the entrance to the California Native collection.

15. Garrya elliptica

Coast silk tassel
Native to California and Oregon

This California native presented me with a glorious show of dripping strands of tiny pink flowers. In springtime, the California Native collection's seven-foot-tall plantings of Garrya elliptica *display tassels that appear like strands of pearls hanging from a wall of green foliage. This is a surprising and superb plant to behold in full bloom and to paint with all its tiny details.*

Lorry Luikart *Artist*

Silk tassel is the perfect common name for this lovely California native. The male catkins, or spikes of flowers, are especially striking with narrow tassels up to eight inches long. The tassels are covered with silky hairs, appearing as though they have been dusted with gold or silver powder. *Garrya elliptica* is dioecious, meaning that male and female reproductive parts occur on separate plants. The inflorescences are beautiful but extremely subtle in color because they are wind pollinated and have no need for brightly colored flowers to attract insect or bird pollinators. Female plants have shorter, thicker tassels up to three inches long. The ripened fruit is a dark purple drupe that resembles a berry. These fruits can stain one's hand and also be a source of natural dye for grey to black.

Garrya elliptica is among the earliest blooming California plants. Flowering as early as December, it is the harbinger of spring in the midst of winter. In its native habitat, the coast silk tassel can be found in several plant communities, principally in drier coastal California and southern Oregon, but usually no more than twenty miles from the ocean. The main associations are coastal scrub, chaparral and mixed evergreen forest.

Various selections have been made from wild forms. The cultivars 'James Roof' and 'Evie' have particularly long catkins, with those of 'James Roof' reaching up to fourteen inches. Usually only male plants are available in the nursery trade as they have the longest and showiest catkins. Most of the specimens in the Botanical Garden can be found in the California Native collection.

16. *Fremontodendron* 'California glory'

Flannel bush

Garden origin: Rancho Santa Ana Botanic Garden, Claremont, California

As a docent at the Bay Area's Regional Parks Botanic Garden, I am particularly interested in painting California native plants. Fremontodendron *has long been one of my favorite native shrubs. The bright yellows, oranges and reds of the blossoms against the dark green leaves are fabulous. Though it seems to bloom all year, 'California Glory' is definitely a must-see when in full bloom in late spring. It glows. I fell in love with one of the Botanical Garden's specimens that is covered with various lichens. It makes me think of a wise old gnome. What stories it would tell us if only it could talk.*

Dolores Morrison *Artist*

Anyone who has seen this plant in full bloom would understand why it was given its cultivar name, 'California Glory'. It is indeed a glory to behold and a plant that is highly sought after for native plant gardens. The profusion of three-inch flowers creates a blanket of color in any landscape. In the wild, *Fremontodendron* can be found sporadically in the coastal ranges, but more frequently in the Sierra Nevada foothills.

This cultivar is a hybrid between two widespread species in California, *F. californicum* and *F. mexicanum,* which is limited to southern California and Baja California. These two species are difficult to grow in cultivation, but the hybrid is vigorous, fast growing, and a bit less sensitive to overwatering. Even so, a single heavy watering around the trunk on a hot summer day has been known to kill it, especially on flat ground where water can pool. Fremontodendrons are best planted in a location away from paths, where they will not require pruning, because the leaves are covered with tiny hairs that irritate the skin when touched. A good location to grow fremontodendrons would be on a hillside in well-drained soil where the flower display can be admired from a distance. Most specimens in cultivation live for only about ten years. There are many lovely examples in the California Native collection.

17. Colletia paradoxa

Anchor plant
Native to southern Brazil, Argentina and Uruguay

A succulent of possibly unique shape, the stems look like leaves and come in pairs at successive right angles, and each stem is crowned with a substantial thorn, making it impossible to approach from any angle. When examined closely, it is a bizarre modern sculpture. When not examined closely, you may feel it before you see it.

Michael Hanley *Artist*

Colletia paradoxa is distinguished by its complex arrangement of vicious looking thorns. A relative of the California lilac (*Ceanothus*), it is visually arresting and wonderfully fragrant in bloom, but it would be a mistake to get too close. The thorns are actually two-inch-wide, triangular spine-tipped modified stems, and are arranged in pairs looking like little ship's anchors, thus the common name. This species is native to southern Brazil, Uruguay and Argentina, where it grows slowly to a shrub eight feet tall and equally as wide.

Although it is not readily available in nurseries, the anchor plant's succulent growth form, low water requirement and frost hardiness make it an ideal barrier plant for much of California. It should never be planted too close to walkways and foot traffic as its defensive spines rival the spiniest cactus.

The plants in the Botanical Garden bloom reliably every summer with beautiful masses of tiny white flowers resembling *Ceanothus*. They provide a sweet scent throughout the west section of the Succulent Garden, often eliciting questions from visitors. Butterflies within range of the scent visit in search of the nectar reward. Almost ten feet tall and more than forty years old, the plants stand near the top of the Succulent Garden like guards, armed and ready.

18. *Lapageria rosea*

Chilean bellflower
Native to Chile

The Lapageria rosea *was a challenge to capture in watercolor because its rosy red flowers have a unique waxy quality. You must seek out these flowers hanging deep among twisted vines that climb over a large tree stump in the Andean Cloud Forest.*

Blue Murov *Artist*

The Chilean bellflower is considered by many to be among the most beautiful of flowering vines. It is the only species in the genus *Lapageria.* The evergreen leaves are a glossy dark green and quite elegant. The three-inch-long, bell-shaped flowers are an inch across, have a waxy texture and are long lasting. The flowers are usually rose-red with netted markings, although other colors have been selected, including pure white and a picotee form – white with crimson edges. The fleshy part of the inch-long fruit is edible and full of seeds.

Lapageria rosea is the national flower of Chile, where it is commonly called Copihue, an indigenous Mapuche word. It grows in forests in the southern part of Chile where it is pollinated by hummingbirds. At one time, *L. rosea* was commonly sold in farmers markets, but is now considered endangered in the wild and is protected by Chilean law.

San Francisco Botanical Garden's climate is perfect for growing this exquisite plant, which is considered by many garden enthusiasts to be quite difficult to grow. The Chilean bellflower prefers partial shade, acidic well-drained soil, and a cool frost-free climate, although it is known to recover from twenty-five degree frosts. The vine is best displayed when it is trained on a trellis or espaliered on the side of a building to show off the pendulous flowers. There are several showy specimens trained onto the west side of the County Fair Building and on the Library courtyard fence. *Lapagaria rosea* can also be found in the Chile collection and the Andean Cloud Forest, where it is often hidden from view as it climbs understory trees, a more accurate representation of how it grows in its native habitat.

19. Brugmansia sanguinea

Red angel's trumpet
Native to South America

While looking for passion flowers along the northern fence of the Botanical Garden, my eyes were inevitably drawn to the group of Brugmansia *in the Andean Cloud Forest. The color of the flowers – with green merging into yellow and then into red – haunted me, and I knew I had to paint that plant in its various stages.*

Terese Bartholomew *Artist*

Brugmansia sanguinea, or red angel's trumpet, with its combination of blood red and canary yellow flowers, is one of the most colorful flowering shrubs in cultivation. The fragrant, eight-inch long tubular red and yellow "trumpets" hang in abundance from horizontal branches like ornaments. This species is native to the cloud forests of the Andes, in the high elevation headwaters of the Amazon River from Colombia, Ecuador and Peru, to northern Bolivia.

Cloud forests, unlike rain forests, have cool temperatures and are at high enough elevations to be shrouded often in clouds. Foggy coastal California is a perfect home for plants from this environment and for this species. This *Brugmansia* requires cool nighttime temperatures to set bud, but cannot withstand a heavy frost, conditions met by the Botanical Garden's coastal California climate. The lower elevation species of *Brugmansia,* with wider flowers, are accustomed to more heat and are beloved garden plants in the southern United States, especially southern California. By contrast, *B. sanguinea* is most successful if grown in coastal California and in its native habitat. In the Botanical Garden, *B. sanguinea* and its cultivars are understory shrubs found mainly in the Andean Cloud Forest.

All *Brugmansia* plant parts have powerful toxic chemicals that can be deadly to animals and humans if ingested. Two of the most potent chemicals in *Brugmansia* are scopolamine and atropine, both known to cause deadly side effects if used inappropriately. Shamans in Peru, practiced and adept at diluting and combining plants so that the chemicals are at safe levels, use *B. sanguinea* in healing rituals.

20. *Syzygium smithii*

Lilly pilly tree
Native to Australia

Who could resist a tree named "lilly pilly" or its joyful clusters of berries showing off in pinks, mauves and deep purple? Add its majestic presence and shimmering leaves, and I was hooked.

Nancy Cohrs *Artist*

Syzygium smithii, the lilly pilly tree, is native to Australian rainforests but thrives in coastal California. With its aromatic leaves and small white flowers, the lilly pilly is an attractive tree. Its most striking feature, however, is the bountiful one-half inch fruit that hangs in clusters in massive displays from autumn into winter. The fruit is produced in such abundance that its weight sometimes can cause the branches to break. The color of the fruit can vary from white to deep maroon. The Botanical Garden is fortunate to have trees with bright lavender fruit that is quite showy.

Visitors often ask if the fruit is edible. Although it has a spongy texture and is not very tasty when eaten raw, the fruit is not toxic and is sometimes used in jams. Many Australian visitors say that the trees in the Botanical Garden are the most spectacular specimens they have seen. In its native habitat, the lilly pilly is often a sparse, poorly formed tree. It can be grown as a specimen tree or pruned more formally as a hedge. Planted over sixty years ago, the Garden's trees have been allowed to grow naturally and are located a short walk from the north entrance, the Friend Gate.

21. Banksia serrata

Old man banksia
Native to Australia

*I was inspired to paint the old man banksia about five years ago when
I came around a bend in the path in the Australian Garden to discover these
extraordinary seed pods embedded in a profusion of hairy, dried stamens.
It was a painter's memorable moment.*

Mary L. Harden *Artist*

Banksia serrata is referred to as old man banksia primarily because of the
whiskered looking "cones," but also because of the gnarled trunks on mature
trees. These cones, held upright on the branches, are actually mature flower
spikes that have protruding seeds, appearing like noses or chins surrounded
by hairy "whiskers" that are old withered flower parts. The distinctive four- to
six-inch cylindrical cones are silver-grey and covered with cream or golden
ribbons that are the pollen receptors of the many flowers on each spike. These
ribbon-like flower parts wither to become the whiskers of the old man
banksia. Children in Australia use "banksia men" as playthings. Each flower
spike is unique depending on which seeds have matured into what can be
imagined as a nose, chin or eyes. The species name, *serrata,* refers to the
serrated or saw-toothed four-inch-long leaves. In favorable locations, this
banksia can reach fifty feet in height, but more often is stunted and gnarled
in appearance.

Like many plants from Australia, *B. serrata* is adapted to survive natural forest
fires. It has thickened bark for protection, an underground root structure that
stores energy for resprouting, and seeds that require heat and smoke to
germinate. There are about seventy-five species of banksias endemic (native
only) to Australia. *Banksia serrata* is found in open forests along the coasts
and mountains of southeastern Australia.

The Botanical Garden has several *B. serrata* plants that bloom reliably every
spring and summer. One particularly nice specimen, planted in 2004 and now
about eighteen feet tall, can be found in the Australia collection. It is a lovely
surprise to come face to face with this tree when it is in full flower.

22. Camellia reticulata 'Notre Dame'

Camellia

Garden origin: O'Malley Estate, Woodside, California

"Go search for something that just astonishes you," said Mary L. Harden.
Many explorations of the Botanical Garden later, Camellia reticulata
'Notre Dame' was looking down at me from high within its shiny foliage.
The large and vibrant flowers with their voluptuous shape and luscious
colors cried out, "Paint me." Yes, with pleasure.

Dianne Boate *Artist*

Camellias are a much loved and cultivated group of flowering shrubs.
Originally native to eastern and southern Asia, they grow well in temperate
and subtropical areas of the world. When well established, they can tolerate
heat and drought and many can be hardy to below freezing. There are more
than three thousand named cultivars, which range widely in size, form and
flower color.

The cultivar illustrated here, *Camellia reticulata* 'Notre Dame', exemplifies
the beauty inherent in the genus. The flowers are large and peony-like with
a red-pink blush, and have golden anthers with yellow filaments. Flowers sit
at the ends of branches from late winter into spring. The dark green, glossy
foliage is clean and attractive. This hardy shrub can grow to ten feet tall.
'Notre Dame' is the result of crossing two other *Camellia reticulata* cultivars:
'Buddha' and 'William Hertrich'.

The Botanical Garden has almost three hundred fifty different camellias.
They are a highlight of our woodland gardens and come into full bloom just
as the magnolias are finishing, bridging the gap between winter and spring
flowers. The most recent addition to the Garden's camellia collection was
the completion of the Camellia Garden across from the Moon Viewing
Garden. The majority of the plants were installed in 2005, when two
hundred mature camellia plants were donated by Bill and Sonja Davidow
from the estate of Marjorie O'Malley. The Camellia Garden was planted
with an emphasis on species to show the wide diversity in the genus *Camellia*.

23. *Protea* 'Pink Ice'

Protea
Genus native to tropical and southern Africa

My interest in botanical illustration is inspired by my love of gardening. Observing and experimenting with drawing and painting plants puts me in touch with the miracle of growth, and provides me with endless visual patterns and forms to explore. The Fibonacci spiral of the protea's dried flower head inspired and perplexed me. It is fascinating that each petal of this plant grows in succession around an apex. The seed capsules form and fit into the gaps left by the first to develop, creating an intersection of spirals. Nature's use of this form in so many contexts amazes me.

Patricia Compton *Artist*

The protea family (Proteaceae) is large and diverse and occurs throughout the southern hemisphere. The family is well represented in the Botanical Garden with many *Leucadendron, Banksia, Leucospermum, Grevillea* and *Protea* in the collection. The genus *Protea* occurs only in tropical and southern Africa, where there are roughly one hundred forty species.

Protea 'Pink Ice' is a hybrid between two species. Horticulturalists agree that *P. susannae* is one parent, while the other parent is thought by some to be *P. compacta* and by others to be *P. nerifolia*. 'Pink Ice' is an outstanding plant for horticulture. The large, five-inch pink flowers have what appears to be a white frosting on the edges of the bracts as well as in the center, creating the illusion of a flower gilded by frost. The five-foot-tall shrub blooms in late winter through spring. The cut flowers last for a month or more and are often used in dried arrangements.

Most proteas are quite sensitive to frost and soil type. *Protea* 'Pink Ice' is considered the most cold hardy of all proteas, tolerating low temperatures close to twenty degrees Fahrenheit. It is also less sensitive to soil type than other members of the genus as long as it is well drained. 'Pink Ice' is just one of many beautiful proteas to be found in the Garden's South Africa collection.

24. Leucadendron argenteum

Silver tree
Native to South Africa

*Silver trees greet you throughout the Botanical Garden with a glimmer of
bright, white light that catches your eye and draws your attention to its source.
It is aptly named the silver tree for its velvety silver-white leaves covered with
tiny hairs that reflect the light. While working on my painting, these shiny
whites continually eluded me until I discovered all the colors of the rainbow
bouncing from leaf to leaf.*

Margaret Barr *Artist*

Leucadendron argenteum, the silver tree, is rarely seen in cultivation in the
United States, largely because of its precise cultural requirements. It is frost
sensitive, prefers acidic soil and needs a dry summer. Most years our
mediterranean climate is perfect for these trees and large specimens have
graced the Botanical Garden. In the occasional hard and prolonged frost,
they will die back and then later resprout and grow. The silver color comes
from the silky hairs covering the leaves that reflect light and capture moisture.
This reflective silvery color is more intense during warm dry periods when
the plants look almost shiny white.

Leucadendron argenteum is considered rare and endangered in its native
habitat of South Africa. Almost one thousand trees can be found at
Kirstenbosch National Botanical Garden in Cape Town, South Africa.
They constitute almost half of the entire wild population, with the rest
growing within a few miles of that garden.

Silver trees are in the protea family and are dioecious, either male or female.
Most of San Francisco Botanical Garden's original plants were male. Now,
however, mature female plants are beginning to develop seedpods that look
like small cones. A good example of these female seedpods can be found
on the large specimen in the Entry Garden. There is also a beautiful male
tree behind the Library building, and many others are located in the South
Africa collection. As with most members of the protea family, silver trees
have become adapted to fire and are usually short lived; for a plant to live
longer than fifty years is very rare. The Botanical Garden plans to develop
a population of both male and female plants, which will allow the Garden
to harvest its own seed and keep these stunning trees in perpetuity.

25. *Leptospermum scoparium* cv.

New Zealand tea tree
Species native to New Zealand and southeastern Australia

This is the plant that keeps on giving. In my garden and San Francisco Botanical Garden, the tea tree brings joy throughout the year. Each season's growth adds another layer of drama. When it seems that nothing else is in flower, you will find tiny tea tree blossoms to cheer you.

Peggy McIntyre *Artist*

The New Zealand tea tree has been grown in California gardens for many decades. Old picturesque forms trained to be small trees with gnarled trunks often can be seen in front of buildings in older neighborhoods around the Bay Area. *Leptospermum scoparium* cultivars can be extremely colorful and showy, and many, from prostrate forms to small trees reaching ten feet tall or more, have been named over the years. The flowers, which can be single or double, range in color from white to pink to red.

Native to New Zealand and southeastern Australia, the species has white flowers and broader leaves than we commonly see on cultivars. Called Manuka by the native Maoris, it is thought that the New Zealand tea tree was the plant that Captain Cook brewed into a tea to prevent his crew from getting scurvy on his voyages of exploration of the South Pacific. The Australian tea tree, *Leptospermum laevigatum,* with its handsome small grey-green leaves, white flowers and twisted trunks, is a common sight in Golden Gate Park. As an example of how common names are often confusing, the plant used for tea tree oil products is a *Melaleuca,* which is also called tea tree.

The cultivar illustrated here has needle-like leaves and is covered with one-half-inch-wide deep pink flowers, which bloom from mid-spring into summer and are reminiscent of miniature roses. Many plants of several *L. scoparium* cultivars can be seen growing in the Botanical Garden by the iron fence that surrounds the west side of Fountain Plaza and down below on either side of the Helene Strybing bench. One particularly nice form with larger than usual flowers and a long blooming season is named 'Helene Strybing', after the generous donor whose founding gift established Strybing Arboretum.

26. Metrosideros excelsa

New Zealand Christmas tree
Native to New Zealand

The minute I saw the crimson tendrils that distinguish the aerial roots descending gracefully from the branches of this gentle giant, I knew I needed to paint it. The paradox for me was figuring out how to convey the enormity of the tree while still showing the tiny details that make the New Zealand Christmas tree such a treasure.

Linda Cavanaugh *Artist*

Metrosideros excelsa, the New Zealand Christmas tree, is called Pohutukawa by the native Maori, who use its dark hard wood "rata" for sculptures. The prolific red bottlebrush-like flowers appear in midsummer, coinciding with the Christmas holidays in the southern hemisphere. The flower petals are actually insignificant; it is the bright red stamens that stand out on these graceful looking dome-shaped trees. The undersides of the leaves are covered in dense white hairs, which add to the tree's striking appearance. In coastal California the showy flowers appear in August. Formerly a favored San Francisco street tree because of its tolerance of ocean wind, it is no longer recommended due to its potentially invasive roots that can lift sidewalks.

Planted before the Botanical Garden began tracking plant records in 1958, the Garden has several mature specimens, including two on the western edge of the McBean Wildfowl Pond that are nearly seventy feet tall. The presence of San Francisco's coastal fog has allowed them to send down red-tipped aerial roots that stretch all the way to the ground to form buttresses. These roots most likely develop to provide support along sea cliffs in their native New Zealand. Inside the Main Gate, near the Library Terrace, there is a rare yellow-flowering form with accompanying yellow-tipped aerial roots that was planted in 1964.

Lorinda Kavanaugh

27. Araucaria araucana

Monkey puzzle tree
Native to Chile and Argentina

I love the patterning of the stiff, sharp, whorled Araucaria araucana *leaves. As an accountant, I am intrinsically drawn to paint plants with strong mathematical sequencing, such as this amazing Fibonacci spiral of 1, 1, 2, 3, 5, 8, 13, 21. I wanted to paint the story of the changing environment that is revealed through the positioning of closer, smaller groups of leaves, which grow during leaner periods. The larger, looser leaves grow during the periods of full sun and sufficient rain preferred by the monkey puzzle tree.*

Jill Petersen *Artist*

Araucaria araucana, the national tree of Chile, is called monkey puzzle tree for good reason. Even the most agile monkey would have a hard time negotiating the spiny leaves of this unusual looking conifer. As young trees, they are symmetrical with layered impenetrable branches covered with overlapping bright green spine-tipped leaves. As *Araucaria* begin to reach maturity, they lose their lower branches and can reach one hundred feet in height, with umbrella-shaped crowns that are quite picturesque. The best specimen in San Francisco Botanical Garden is a young twenty-foot tree on the lawn between the Friend Gate and the McBean Wildfowl Pond.

This wind-pollinated species is dioecious, meaning that each tree has only male or female reproductive parts. The female trees produce a very large cone that can have up to two hundred seeds, which are edible and similar to large pine nuts. The seeds were a food source of the Araucanians, the early indigenous people of central Chile. Mostly logged for timber in their native habitat, monkey puzzle trees are now considered rare and endangered. *Araucaria araucana* is the most cold hardy of the species in this genus.

Located just north of the Zellerbach Garden, the oldest *Araucaria*, *A. angustifolia*, is starting to assume the umbrella-shaped characteristic of mature trees in this genus. As landscape plants, they are best utilized in large estates or parks where they can be viewed from a safe distance. When mature, they produce large, heavy cones the size of bowling balls, indicating another common name, widow maker, as the falling cones can be dangerous. Gardening under *Araucaria* is difficult, since fallen leaves remain spiny for many years.

28. Gunnera tinctoria

Chilean rhubarb

Native to Chile and Argentina

How could you not love a huge Gunnera? *The leaves are as big as a three-foot umbrella, and grow out of a swirled spring topknot. The gigantic, crinkled, dried leaves are veined, gnarled, and a wonderful inspiration for me to paint their exuberance. Dinosaurs would have loved this plant.*

Yvonne Goldman *Artist*

Gunnera tinctoria, with its massive lobed and toothed leaves, can grow to eight feet tall and just as wide in a single season. Formerly named *Gunnera chilensis,* its common name is Chilean rhubarb. The large flaring leaf blades are held nearly upright, reflecting another common name for this plant, poor man's umbrella. The two-foot-tall conical flower stalk appears in early summer and remains until the plant dies back in the winter. The flowering stalk can have thousands of tiny, densely packed flowers that turn into reddish oblong fruit. The stem-like petioles of the new leaves in spring can be peeled and eaten raw or cooked as a spring vegetable and have an acidic and refreshing flavor.

The plants need plenty of water and can be found near streams, ponds and other wetland areas. Once established, *G. tinctoria* is very robust and considered invasive in some areas. An individual plant can be quite a conversation piece, while a large cluster, like those lining the stream north of the Ancient Plant Garden, gives the feeling of walking in a prehistoric wonderland. This is one reason why these plants are grown in the Ancient Plant Garden even though there is some debate about the development of this genus, which is considered modern to some botanists and primitive to others. According to Eric Walther, first director of Strybing Arboretum, the plants in the Botanical Garden were originally grown from seed from the Inverness, California garden of Hugh Logan, an avid Bay Area gardener who died in 1961.

29. *Magnolia grandiflora*

Southern magnolia

Native to the southeastern United States

I have always been inspired to paint the magnolia, with its luscious, leathery leaves and magnificent large white flowers. Magnolia grandiflora *grabbed my attention with its hundreds of greens, and the brown undersides of the leaves, each more interesting than the next. This was difficult to paint because the large, creamy-white flowers faded quickly. I simply could not resist.*

Nancy J. Ballard *Artist*

Magnolia grandiflora, or southern magnolia, is widely associated with the southern United States and was the emblem of the Confederacy. Its natural range is from coastal North Carolina to eastern Texas, where it can be found at the edges of bodies of water such as rivers, tidelands and swamps. Highly adaptable, the tree is now planted as far north as Chicago to southern New York, and up and down the West Coast. In forested areas, it can grow up to one hundred feet, although in open and windy habitats it tends to remain shorter and shrub-like. The southern magnolia is the state flower of Mississippi and Louisiana, and ranks among the noblest of North American broad-leaved trees.

The attractive white flowers can be as large as one foot in diameter. They appear in spring and summer, their creamy white tepals contrasting dramatically with the dark glossy evergreen foliage. The large shiny leaves make beautiful winter wreaths and long-lasting floral arrangements. Over one hundred cultivars, with a wide range of sizes and leaf textures, have been named.

Across from the Ancient Plant Garden, there are two large specimens, planted more than fifty years ago. The cultivar 'Samuel Sommer', on the north side of the Great Meadow, has striking cinnamon brown felt on the undersides of its leaves.

30. *Rhododendron* 'John McLaren'

Rhododendron

Garden origin: Golden Gate Park, San Francisco, California

Rhododendron 'John McLaren' called out to me and I saw the possibility of a love affair. A large bud looked like an artichoke sitting in a circle of lush green leaves. There was a speck of red peeking out of the bud that made me curious about the flower. After four days of painting, I discovered that the bud had burst into a huge bouquet of small red to magenta flowers. Little did I know that this painterly love affair would last for a year as I brought this composition to fruition.

Judy Mac *Artist*

John McLaren, the first superintendent of Golden Gate Park, loved rhododendrons. He supervised the original plantings in the Park and served as superintendent for fifty years. In 1887, seven varieties of rhododendron were planted in Golden Gate Park. By 1893, McLaren had added mass plantings of forty-four more varieties, and by 1910, the number had grown to eighty-five. As a memorial to his love of rhododendrons, a section of the Park across from the Conservatory of Flowers was named the John McLaren Memorial Rhododendron Dell.

There are over eight hundred fifty species of rhododendrons distributed widely around the world except for South America and Africa. The highest species diversity is found in Asia. Over 28,000 cultivars are in the International Rhododendron Registry held by the Royal Horticultural Society. Currently, the Botanical Garden has over three hundred fifty different rhododendrons.

Among the hybrids and seedlings planted in the Rhododendron Dell was a very floriferous, unnamed seedling that was eventually given the name *Rhododendron* 'John McLaren'. It is a large rhododendron that blooms prolifically with flowers that seem to glow and resemble large soft roses. The Botanical Garden's most striking specimen was planted in 1991 and is now ten feet tall. It is one of the first to bloom in the Rhododendron Garden each year, sometimes as early as December, providing a showy and beautiful beginning to the rhododendron blooming season.

Acknowledgements

The *Treasures from San Francisco Botanical Garden at Strybing Arboretum* catalog, the *Treasures* map and the thirty-piece art exhibition have involved the goodwill and collaboration of many individuals and institutions.

A special thanks to Mary L. Harden, Director of the Botanical Illustration Program, for envisioning and creating the *Treasures* map, for envisioning the exhibition catalog, for providing the use of the *Banksia serrata*, *Ardisia venosa* and map images, and for curating and hanging the art exhibition.

The artistic production depends entirely upon the creative talents of the botanical Master Artists who have provided their images for the map and the catalog: Juanita Alexander, Nancy J. Ballard, Roslyn Banish, Margaret Barr, Terese Bartholomew, Dianne Boate, Jo Boero, Linda Cavanaugh, Nancy Cohrs, Patricia Compton, Catherine Dellor, Yvonne Goldman, Michael Hanley, Mary Ann Ho, Jane Kraft, Lorry Luikart, Judy Mac, Martha McClaren, Peggy McIntyre, Dolores Morrison, Blue Murov, Rosemary O'Connell, Jill Petersen, Mary Plovanic, Stephanie Tarczy, Kate Townsend, Amber Turner, and Katie Young.

We wish to acknowledge the generous support of Igor Sokoloff, framing to ASBA standards; Jay Daniel of Black Cat Studios, art digitalization and print production; Helene Sobol, publication consultant and graphic design; Linda Cavanaugh of Coastal Art Services, graphic services; Dianne Boate, publicity, and San Francisco Parks Alliance for the Botanical Illustration Program sponsorship.

We would also like to extend our gratitude to Robert Meyer, Nick Bovis, Margaret Barr, and Julie Allecta, who generously contributed to the exhibition.

A number of individuals from San Francisco Botanical Garden Society contributed to the project. The plant descriptions in the *Treasures* catalog were researched, written and edited collaboratively by the Botanical Garden Society's Curator, Dr. Don Mahoney, Associate Curator David Kruse-Pickler, Head Librarian Brandy Kuhl, and Molley Lowry, longtime docent, Art Exhibits Coordinator and member of the Library's Art Exhibits Selection Committee. Mona Bourell, Plant Collections Registrar, and Lee Boerger, botanical artist and member of the Art Exhibits Selection Committee, also assisted with the catalog. Oversight of the exhibition and coordination of the catalog text were provided by Brandy Kuhl, with support from Molley Lowry. The curatorial staff provided plant names, locations and signage for the map and walk; in addition to those already mentioned, we thank Curatorial Assistant Marc Johnson.

Many thanks to Dr. Frank Almeda, Chairman and Senior Curator for Botany at California Academy of Sciences, for his helpful review and comment on the plant descriptions. We also thank Margo Bors for allowing us to use her portrait of Barbara Pitschel.

Funding for production and publishing of the catalog and *Treasures* map was provided by San Francisco Botanical Garden Society for the benefit of the Helen Crocker Russell Library of Horticulture. Thank you to Executive Director Sue Ann L. Schiff for editorial support and guiding the project to completion.

All partners appreciate the collaborative relationship with the San Francisco Recreation and Park Department.